The Apostolic Pardon

The Plenary Indulgence at the Time of Death

Rev. James O'Kane

Edited by Fr. Chad Ripperger, Ph.D.

Nihil Obstat: Father Cliff Ermatinger, S.T.L. Ph.L
Censor Librorum

Imprimatur: + Most Reverend Samuel J. Aquila, S.T.L.
Archbishop of Denver
Denver, Colorado, USA
December 15, 2024

The *Nihil Obstat* and *Imprimatur* are official declarations that a book or a pamphlet is free from doctrinal or moral error. No implication is contained therein that those who have granted the *Nihil Obstat* and *Imprimatur* agree with the contents, opinions or statements expressed.

In Honor of All of the Holy Pontiffs

Table of Contents

Introduction ... vii

The Apostolic Pardon ... 1

Rite to Be Observed by Priests Delegated to Give the Apostolic Benediction "In Articulo Mortis." ... 3

Appendix:
    Current Requirements for a Plenary Indulgence ... 19

The Apostolic Pardon

RITE TO BE OBSERVED BY PRIESTS DELEGATED TO GIVE THE APOSTOLIC BENEDICTION "IN ARTICULO MORTIS."

RITUS BENEDICTIONIS APOSTOLICÆ IN ARTICULO MORTIS A SACERDOTIBUS AD ID DELEGATIS IMPERTIENDÆ.[5]

955. This title or chapter is not found in any of the rituals published before the time of Benedict XIV, for it was he who prescribed the present formula. From the earliest ages of the Church bishops were invited, from time to time, to give their blessing to the dying,[6] and when given by the popes, or those especially delegated by them, it was, no doubt, very often accompanied by a plenary indulgence. We have, most probably, an instance of this in the indulgence granted to St. Clare by Innocent IV, as we read in her life given in the Roman Breviary.[7] At all events, it is certain that the popes have power to grant such indulgences, and that this power has been frequently used in the Church.[8]

956. Before the time of Benedict XIV, they readily granted to

---

[5]Ed.: This text is taken from chapter XVII (pp. 465-474) of *Notes on the Rubrics of the Roman Ritual* by Rev. James O'Kane (James Duffy and Co. Limited. Dublin. 1922.).

[6]Catalani, tit. V. cap. cap. vi n. ii.

[7]Catal., l. c.

[8]See Bouvier, *Traité de Indulgences*, part. ii, cap. ii.

bishops the faculty of giving, by themselves, or by priests, whom they were permitted to delegate in special cases, a benediction with plenary indulgence to the sick "in articulo mortis." But this great pope, in the bull, "*Pia mater,*" etc., extended the faculty very considerably. In view of recent legislation the extension granted need not be mentioned now. The pope at the same time pointed out that care should be taken in catechisms and public instructions to explain to the people the doctrine of the Church with regard to the temporal punishment due to sin; the obligation of satisfying God's justice, by fasting, alms, prayers, and other good works; and the danger of presumptuously relying on the efficacy of the sacrament of Penance and a plenary indulgence at the hour of death; for, he says, it is uncertain what kind our death may be, whether we shall receive the plenary indulgence at that last moment whether, even in case the external rite be applied, we shall reap the fruit of it, or to what extent we shall be benefitted by it.

He prescribes that all priests who have to assist the dying, and apply to them this indulgence "in articulo mortis," shall excite them to sorrow for their sins, and inspire them with sentiments of fervent love of God and perfect resignation to His holy will, so as to accept death from His hand in punishment for their sins. It is this disposition especially which he requires in order that they may gain the fruit of the indulgence. "Hoc enim praecipue opus in hujusmodi articulo constitutis imponimus et injungimus, quo se ad indulgentiae plenariae fructum consequendum, praeparent atque disponant."[9]

---

[9]Trans.: "For this particular work we lay down and enjoin in the constitutions of this article, by which they prepare and arrange themselves in order to obtain the fruit of a plenary indulgence."

Introduction

The Catholic doctrine on purgatory, defined by the Council of Trent,[1] constitutes a rich reflection for all "wayfarers," that is, those in this life on their way to their final eternal destination. Precious few bypass purgatory; according to Catholic theology, only martyrs and the perfect manage not to spend time in purgatory. The perfect have no need of time in purgatory, because they have already been purged of all of their imperfections, necessary to enter heaven, since no one can enter into the company of God with the slightest blemish on his soul. The martyrs, by a special grace of God, sustain death for the faith or heroic Christian virtue, and in laying down their life sacrifice by surrendering everything they are and have in this life, thereby expiating for the temporal punishment due to their sins.

The profundity of the divine mercy that God has for men is magnificently demonstrated in the conferring to St. Peter and his successors the keys over the spiritual treasury of the Church, so that by their word,[2] the faithful can obtain from that spiritual treasury the application of the sufferings of Christ to the atonement for the temporal punish due to their sin and, hence, be granted a full pardon for having violated divine

---

[1] Session 25.

[2] Matthew 16:17-19: "And Jesus answering said to him: Blessed art thou, Simon Bar-Jona: because flesh and blood hath not revealed it to thee, but my Father who is in heaven. And I say to thee: That thou art Peter; and upon this rock I will build my church, and the gates of hell shall not prevail against it. And I will give to thee the keys of the kingdom of heaven. And whatsoever thou shalt bind upon earth, it shall be bound also in heaven: and whatsoever thou shalt loose on earth, it shall be loosed also in heaven."

justice. The Church's doctrine on indulgences brings great solace to those whose spiritual advance is such that they have a sensitivity to their obligation to pay back for what they have stolen from God's glory in their life by their sin, and the necessity to render their souls in a state of perfection,[3] before the mighty judgment seat of God.

At the time of death, one is at the doorstep of a true reckoning for one's life. What great compassion God has in giving the Church the power to wipe away all of the restitution one must pay back to Him. A plenary indulgence at the time of death is truly a manifestation of God's love for man and His desire that in this life we dwell under His mercy, so that we may enjoy in eternity the reality that "His mercy endures forever."[4]

A renewed interest in obtaining a plenary indulgence at the time of one's death has arisen. The Church's granting of what is known as the Apostolic Pardon or Apostolic Blessing is, again, being sought by the faithful...of those that are even aware of it. It is with great sadness that the teaching about this indulgence fell into disuse among the clergy shortly after Vatican II, largely due to neglect on the side of priests, but also due to a progressive belief that everyone is saved, and it is not necessary to anoint them on their death bed, let alone give them the pardon. An attitude of "God understands" overtook many in the Church, leading to the error that God forgives absolutely everything without condition or requirement on our part. As a result, seminarians were not taught in the seminary about the Apostolic Pardon for decades

---

[3] Matthew 5:48; " Be you therefore perfect, as also your heavenly Father is perfect."

[4] Psalms 117 and 135.

and priests would often learn about it only after they had been ordained for some time.

This book provides a short summary of the Church's teachings on the Apostolic Pardon or Blessing. Hopefully, the faithful in being aware of it can request it for themselves, when dying, or for their loved ones when they are passing. It is with this hope that the book is published, so that due pastoral solicitude can be given to those who are faithfully departing.

The text of O'Kane is provided with virtually no editing to the body of the text. Slight edits were made to the footnotes for stylistic reasons. The footnotes were also renumbered to include editorial comments as well as translations of sections of the Latin he quotes. The paragraph numbers are from the original text and included here for reference for those who wish to reference his original work.

Lastly, to leave nothing undecided, he prescribed the formula here given in the ritual to be used in the application of the indulgence.

> § I—Benedictio in articulo mortis cum soleat impertiri post Sacramenta Poenitentiæ, Eucharistiæ, et Extremæ Unctionis illis infirmis, qui vel illam petierint, dum sana mente et integris sensibus erant, seu verisimiliter petiissent, vel dederint signa contritionis; impertienda iisdem est, etiamsi postea linguae, caeterorumque sensuum usu sint destituti, aut in delirium vel amentiam inciderint. Excommunicatis vero, impoenitentibus, et qui in manifesto peccato mortali moriuntur, est omnino deneganda.[10]

957. The circumstances in which the benediction is to be given or refused, as here stated, are evidently the same as those in which Extreme Unction is to be given or refused. It may be doubted, however, whether the benediction is restricted, like Extreme Unction, to such as are in danger of death from bodily sickness, whether it may not be given to one who is in danger of death from any other cause, *e.g.*, to a convict about to be executed? The words of the bull, "*Pia mater*," as well as of the rubrics here, undoubtedly seem to suppose that the

---

[10]Trans.: "The blessing at the time of death is usually imparted after the Sacraments of Penance, Eucharist, and Extreme Unction to those sick who have either asked for it while they were of sound mind and senses, or are likely to have asked, or have given signs of contrition; it must be imparted to them, even if afterwards they are destitute of the use of the tongue, and of the other senses, or fall into delirium or insanity. As for the excommunicated, the impenitent, and those who die in manifest mortal sin, it is absolutely to be denied."

person receiving the benediction is "ægrotus, infirmus,"[11] etc. The Propaganda,[12] however, replied that the blessing may be given "damnatis ad mortem, dum ad illam subeundam ducuntur, vel eadem die qua eam subituri sunt."[13]

958. The Sacred Congregation decided that this benediction should be given to children who are thought too young to be admitted to Holy Communion.[14] What has been said regarding the administration of Extreme Unction to children applies also to the benediction.

The question of course regards children who have attained the use of reason; otherwise, being incapable of sinning, they would be also incapable of receiving an indulgence.

959. It is certain that the benediction may generally be repeated in the circumstances in which Extreme Unction may be repeated, that is, when the sick person, having partially recovered, relapses, and is again in danger of death. But in a case of protracted illness it cannot be lawfully repeated, even though it would be lawful to repeat the sacrament of Extreme Unction.[15] If, however, the person recovered from his illness

---

[11]Trans.: "sick, weak."

[12]Ed.: That is, the Congregation for the Propagation of the Faith (S.C.R.).

[13]Trans.: "condemned to death, while they are being led to undergo it, or on the same day on which they are to undergo it."

[14]S.C.R., *Decr. auth.,* n. 2650, 16 Dec. 1826.

[15]S.C.I., *Decr. auth.,* n. 257, ad vii. 3o.

and afterwards "quacumque de causa"[16] incurs a new danger of death, it is lawful to repeat the benediction.[17]

It had been long before decided by the same Congregation, that a plenary indulgence "in articulo mortis" given simply and without any other declaration, should be understood strictly, as gained only when death actually occurs.[18] It would be different, of course, if the terms of the brief contained the clause "etiamsi mors non sequatur,"[19] which is contained in some referred to by Bouvier in his discussion of this matter.

960. The benediction is to be given to those who even through their own fault have not received the last sacraments and are now at the point of death,[20] unless, of course, they are manifestly dying in a state of impenitence. The reason is that this indulgence is gained *only at the moment of death*; and even a person who has neglected to receive the last sacraments may, by an act of contrition, render himself capable of gaining the indulgence before death occurs.

961. The benediction is not to be repeated even though the person was actually in the state of mortal sin at the time of its

---

[16]Trans.: "From whatever cause."

[17]Ibid., n. 300.

[18]23 April, 1675, ad 1, n. 8.

[19]Trans.: "even if death does not follow."

[20]23 April, 1675, ad 1, n. 237, ad 5.

reception.[21] And should he, after having received it in the state of grace, again fall into mortal sin, he would receive the fruit of the indulgence at the moment of death, provided he had, in the meantime, recovered the state of grace; and, therefore, in this case also, the benediction should not be repeated.

962. Bouvier observes that in the diocese of Mans, it is usual to give the benediction immediately after Extreme Unction. This, undoubtedly, should be the ordinary rule.[22] It is evident from what is said regarding the dispositions required, that the priest should give it, if possible, while the person has still the full use of his faculties, and should not, therefore, wait till the last moment. If there be no immediate danger, however, and if the priest can conveniently return, it may be sometimes expedient to defer it for another visit.

> §II.—Habens predictam facultatem, ingrediendo cubiculum, ubi jacet infirmus, dicat: *Pax huic domui*, etc., ac deinde aegrotum, cubiculum, et circumstantes aspergat aqua benedicta, dicendo Antiphonam: *Asperges me*, etc.[23]

963. Formerly special delegation was necessary in order that the priest might validly give the benediction. But this is no

---

[21] Ibid., n. 257, ad viii, 1o.

[22] Ed.: This is the general practice of the Church.

[23] Trans.: "Having the aforesaid faculty, entering the room where the sick person lies, he should say: *Peace to this house*, etc., and then sprinkle the sick person, the room, and those around him with blessed water, saying the Antiphon: *Sprinkle me*, etc."

longer so. The Code of Canon Law[24] declares:

> Parocho aliive sacerdoti qui infirmis assistat, facultas est eis concedendi benedictionem apostolicam cum indulgentia plenaria in articulo mortis, secundum formam a probatis liturgicis libris traditam, quam benedictionem impertiri ne omittat.[25]

964. The rubric supposes that the priest comes for the purpose of giving the benediction; and in this case, on entering the room he says, "*Pax huic domui*," and sprinkles the holy water as here directed. De Herdt[26] recommends for greater security that he do go even when he gives the benediction immediately after Extreme Unction, because the rubric occurs in the

---

[24] Ed.: That is, the CIC/1917. The current ritual of the Anointing of the Sick states that the priest "may add the apostolic pardon for the dying" after the penitential rite or after the sacrament of Penance. When Viaticum is given within Mass, "the apostolic pardon may be added after the final blessing." The Apostolic Blessing has two forms in the Ordinary Form for the Anointing of the Sick: Form A: "Through the holy mysteries of our redemption, may Almighty God release you from all punishments in this life and in the life to come. May He open to you the gates of paradise and welcome you to everlasting joy." Form B reads as follows: "By the authority which the Apostolic See has given me, I grant you a full pardon and the remission of all your sins in the name of the Father, and of the Son, (+) and of the Holy Spirit." For the full ritual of the Apostolic Pardon of the Extraordinary Form discussed in this text, see the *Rituale Romanum* (1962), title V, chpt. 6.

[25] Trans.: "A pastor or other priest who assists the sick has the opportunity to grant them the apostolic blessing with a plenary indulgence at the point of death, according to the form handed down by approved liturgical books, which blessing he does not omit to impart."

[26] Pars vi, n. 25, vi.

formula of Benedict XIV, and may therefore express a strict condition of the indulgence. But there can hardly, we think, be a reasonable doubt that in that case, having already said the "*Pax huic domui*," and sprinkled the water on entering the room, he may safely omit the repetition.[27]

965. He should be vested in surplice and violet stole,[28] and therefore should retain the vestments he has used in giving Extreme Unction, if he gives the benediction immediately after.

> §III.– Quod si ægrotus voluerit confiteri, audiat illum, et absolvat. Si confessionem non petat, excitet illum ad eliciendum actum contritionis; de hujus Benedictionis efficacia ac virtute, si tempus ferat, breviter admoneat; tum instruat, atque hortetur, ut morbi incommoda ac dolores in anteactæ vitæ expiationem libenter perferat, Deoque sese paratum offerat ad ultro acceptandum, quidquid ei placuerit, et mortem ipsam patienter obeundam in satisfactionem poenarum, quas peccando promeruit.[29]

---

[27] Ed.: By way of explanation, what O'Kane is observing here is that in the extraordinary form of Extreme Unction or the giving of all of the last rites, the *Pax huic domui* is said at the very beginning of the last rites or when Extreme Unction is given on its own. Hence, if it is already said, it does not have to be repeated.

[28] Caval., vol. iv. cap. xxvii., *De Benedictione in vita et mortis articulo*, Decr. vii. in fine.

[29] Trans.: "But if the sick person wishes to confess, let him hear him, and absolve him. If he does not ask for confession, he will encourage him to elicit an act of contrition; if he has time, let him give a brief admonition of the effectiveness and power of this blessing; then

966. The Church, anxious about the spiritual welfare of her children at every period of their lives, becomes more and more solicitous about them as death approaches, knowing that their salvation depends on their dying in the state of grace. Hence, she is ready to administer to them over and over again, the holy sacrament of Penance, instituted by her Divine Founder as the sovereign remedy for sin. She directs the priest, as often as he visits the sick, to ascertain whether they desire to confess, and if so, to hear and absolve them; and it is her wish that, if possible, he should be present with them in the last agony.

967. St. Ligouri recommends confessors who assist the dying to give them absolution frequently while they have the use of their senses:

> Dum infirmus adhuc sensibus viget, absolutionem pluries ei conferri post brevem reconciliationem juvabit, ut ita ille magis circa statum gratiæ securus reddatur, si forsan præteritæ confessiones invalidæ fuissent, aut saltem gratiæ augmentum recipiat, necnon purgatorii poenæ ei minuantur."[30]

---

he instructs and exhorts him to willingly bear the discomforts and pains of the illness as an atonement for his past life, and to offer himself to God ready to accept whatever He pleases, and to suffer death itself patiently in satisfaction of the punishments which he has earned by sinning."

[30] *Praxis Confess.*, n. 276: "While the sick man is still strong in his senses, it will help him to be absolved several times after a short reconciliation, so that he may be made more secure in his state of grace, if perhaps his past confessions had been invalid, or at least he may receive an increase of grace, and the punishments of purgatory may be lessened."

"Juxta praescriptum et mentem Ritualis Romani," says the Council of Baltimore, "sedulus sit Pastor animarum in visitandis infirmis et agonizantibus etiam postquam ultima receperunt sacramenta; et illos exhortetur, consoletur, adjuvet; et elicito ab iis, si possint, novo confessionis et contritionis actu, nova identidem donet absolutione."[31]

968. In the present case, if the sick person does not confess, the priest should endeavour to excite him to contrition, as is directed not only by the rubric here, but in the bull itself. It does not appear, however, that this is rigorously required as a condition of the indulgence, but it gives greater security that the person is in the state of grace, which is absolutely necessary to gain any indulgence. He should then simply explain to him, if time permits, the efficacy of the benediction he is about to impart, and especially he should exhort him to be patient and resigned to the will of God in his sufferings, and to be ready to accept death in satisfactum for his sins, and as a punishment deserved by them. This is the disposition on which the Pontiff chiefly insists, as we have already seen. The invocation of the sacred Name, mentally at least, if not with the lips, is a *conditio sine qua non* of gaining the indulgence, when the subject is *compos mentis*.[32] If the person has lost the use of speech, or is even apparently unconscious, the priest,

---

[31] Prov. v. Decr. xi.: "According to the precepts and mind of the Roman Ritual, the pastor of souls should be diligent in visiting the sick and dying even after they have received the last sacraments; and he will exhort them, console them, and help them; and elicit from them, if they can, by a new act of confession and contrition, he will again and again grant new absolution."

[32] S. C. I., *Decr. auth.,* n. 237, ad 7 ; also 22 Sept. 1892.

will, therefore, be careful to suggest the invocation of the sacred Name. For it not unfrequently happens that in such circumstances the use of reason is still retained.

> §IV.— Tum piis ipsum verbis consoletur, in spem erigens, fore, ut ex divina munificentia largitate eam poenarum remissionem, et vitam sit consecuturus æternam.[33]

969. He should then console and encourage him, inspiring him with a confident hope of obtaining, through the mercy and goodness of God, a full remission of all his sins, and eternal happiness in the next life. He may use any words which his piety may suggest, but it would be difficult to find any more appropriate than those short sentences given in the ritual itself, in its instructions to the pastor on the mode of assisting the dying.[34]

> §V.— Postea dicit: *Adjutorium nostrum, etc.* Tum dicto ab uno ex Clericis adstantibus *Confiteor, etc.*, Sacerdos dicat: *Misereatur, etc.,* Deinde: *Dominus noster, etc.*[35]

---

[33]Trans. "Then he consoled himself with pious words, raising him to the hope that, by the divine gracious bounty, he would receive remission of punishment and eternal life."

[34]O'Kane, then, proceeds to explain the manner of administering the Apostolic Blessing in the extraordinary form.

[35]Trans.: "Afterwards he says: *Our help, etc.* Then said by one of the clerics standing by: *I confess, etc.*, the priest says: *May the mercy, etc.* Then: *Our Lord, etc.*

970. The form here given is that prescribed by Benedict XIV, and of course should be adhered to in every particular when circumstances permit. It was doubted whether the "*Confiteor*" should be said if the benediction be given immediately after Extreme Unction, since it has been said just before the administration of that sacrament; but the Sacred Congregation of Indulgences decided that it should again he said, the question proposed being, whether it should be recited thrice when the Viaticum, Extreme Unction, and this benediction follow in immediate succession.[36]

971. The priest says "*Misereatur tui*," etc., as in administering the Viaticum, and makes the sign of the cross over the sick person when saying "*In nomine Patris,*" etc., and also at the end, while saying "Pater, Filius", etc.

> §VI.— Si vero infirmus sit adeo morti proximus, ut neque confessionis generalis faciendæ, neque præmissarum, precum recitandarum suppetat tempus, statim Sacerdos Benedictionem ei impertiatur.[37]

972. In ordinary cases it is unlawful to omit any part of the full form, as given in the Ritual. But if it is feared that there

---

[36] 5 Feb. 1841, *in Valentinen*, ad 6 n. dvi. In case of urgency it is sufficient to say the *Confiteor* only once. "Si immineat necessitas conferendi unum post aliud immediate, licere (sc. dicere) semel in casu; secus repetatur" (C.S.Off. 1 Sept. 1851). ("If there is an imminent necessity of conferring one immediately after another, it is permissible (namely, to say) once in a case; otherwise it is repeated.")

[37] Trans.: "If, however, he is so weak that he is so close to death that he has neither time to make a general confession nor to recite the prayers, the priest immediately imparts the blessing to him."

would not be sufficient time to recite the prayers in full, because death is imminent, the priest may, according to a rubric given in the Breviary, commence with the words *Dominus noster*, etc. Further, if the person is at the point of death (*si mors proxime tergeat*), it is sufficient to use the formula: *Indulgentiam plenariam et remissionem omnium peccatorum tibi concedo. In nomine Patris, et Filii, et Spiritus Sancti. Amen.*

973. The Congregation of Rites has declared[38] that this very short form may also be used in case of an epidemic, "ad contagium evitandum."[39] This form is given in the Ritual only as part of the prayer *Dominus noster*, etc. But in the revised edition the words are printed in heavy type in order to emphasize, we suppose, that the form is sufficient in very urgent cases.

974. The Congregation of Indulgences has decided[40] that the benediction may be given to a number together. But the prayer, *Dominus noster*, etc., as far as... "*et Spiritus Sancti. Amen,*" must be said *singulariter singulis.*[41] In the other versicles and prayers the usual changes are to be made in number and, if necessary, gender.

975. It may be observed that this is not the only plenary indulgence that can be obtained at the hour of death. A great

---

[38] *Decr. authen.* S.C.R., n. 3483, 8 Mar. 1879.

[39] Trans.: "in order to avoid contagion."

[40] 10 Jun. 1884.

[41] Trans.: "Individually over each one."

many have been granted for this hour to the faithful who are members of certain pious confraternities, who practice certain devotions, or who have rosaries, crosses, medals, etc., to which the indulgences are attached, provided they comply with the requisite conditions.[42] The titles on which these indulgences are granted are altogether distinct, and the conditions are not incompatible. It has been decided by the Sacred Congregation of Indulgences, that, when Communion is required as a condition of the indulgence, the same Communion may suffice for several plenary indulgences.[43]

976. The conditions required for those granted "in articulo

---

[42]Bouvier, *Traité des Indulgences*, partie ii, chap. ii, Qu. 4.

[43]This paragraph should be read in its historical context, insofar as many of the indulgences that were granted prior to 1968 have been abrogated by Paul VI and superceded by the *Enchiridion Indulgentiarum* issued by the Sacred Apostolic Penitentiary in 1968. The following plenary indulgence is granted according to the Enchiridion:

28
The Moment of Death (In articulo mortis)

To the faithful in danger of death, who cannot be assisted by a priest to bring them the sacraments and impart the Apostolic Blessing with its plenary indulgence (see can. 468, §2 of Code of Canon Law), Holy Mother Church nevertheless grants a *plenary indulgence* to be acquired at the point of death, provided they are properly disposed and have been in the habit of reciting some prayers during their lifetime. The use of a crucifix or a cross to gain this indulgence is praiseworthy.

The condition: *provided they have been in the habit of reciting some prayers during their lifetime* supplies in such cases for the three usual conditions required for the gaining of a plenary indulgence.

The plenary indulgence at the point of death can be acquired by the faithful, even if they have already obtained another plenary indulgence on the same day.

The above grant is taken from the Apostolic Constitution The Doctrine of Indulgences, Norm 18.

mortis" are very easy. They are, for the most part, those acts which should, in any event, be frequently elicited by the Christian in danger of death — acts of contrition, acts of the love of God, and of perfect resignation to His holy will, and the invocation of the sacred Name with the heart, if not with the lips.

To gain the indulgences attached to rosaries, crosses, medals, etc., it is enough to take the blessed object, in the hand, or to have it about or near the person, while making the acts prescribed, which are usually those just mentioned. The ministry of a priest is not necessary, though it is of course very useful in assisting the sick person to make the acts required. It is probable that, even by virtue of a single concession, the indulgence may be gained as often as the prescribed acts are repeated,[44] but there is no reason to doubt that several may be gained when the titles are distinct.[45]

With respect to the intention, it is sufficient that one have that of gaining all the indulgences he can by the acts he performs. It is not necessary to think of them in particular, nor even to know that they are attached to the acts. It is even probable that an intention of gaining the indulgence is not required at all, provided the work to which it is attached be done. St. Ligouri seems to think that, at all events, it is enough to have an interpretative intention.

---

[44] Busemb., apud St. Lig., lib. vi., n. 534 — 4. In view of the various decisions of the Congregation of Indulgences we think this opinion can no longer be sustained. If an indulgence is granted to be gained *in articulo mortis* it can manifestly be gained only once. There is only one *articulus mortis*. (Ed.: The comment in this footnote was made by the editor of O'Kane's text.)

[45] Again, the reader is reminded that the laws governing indulgences were changed in 1969.

977. The priest, then, should not fail to suggest to the sick person this easy yet powerful means of satisfying the divine justice. It is true that if he had the happiness of gaining one plenary indulgence, he could not gain a second for himself at the same time, for even one includes a complete remission of all the temporal punishment due to his sins; but it is hard to reckon in any instance on the presence of all those conditions, and especially of those perfect dispositions which are necessary to gain a plenary indulgence in its full extent. But, although it be not gained in its whole extent, it may be gained partially; and if many be gained in this way, the effect of all united may come very near, and, when there is complete renunciation of all venial sins, may be equal to the full effect of a plenary indulgence.[46]

---

[46]See De Lugo, *De pœnitentia*, Disp. xxvii. sec vi. n. 91.

Appendix:
Current Requirements for a Plenary Indulgence[47]

24. §1. A plenary indulgence can be acquired once only in the course of a day.

§2. But one can obtain the plenary indulgence *for the moment of death*, even if another plenary indulgence had already been acquired on the same day.

§3. A partial indulgence can be acquired more than once a day, unless otherwise expressly indicated.

25. The work prescribed for acquiring a plenary indulgence connected with a church or oratory consists in a devout visit and the recitation during the visit of one *Our Father* and the *Creed*.

26. To acquire a plenary indulgence it is necessary to perform the work to which the indulgence is attached and to fulfill the following three conditions: sacramental confession, eucharistic Communion, and prayer for the intention of the Sovereign Pontiff. It is further required that all attachment to sin, even venial sin, be absent.

If the latter disposition is in any way less than perfect or if the prescribed three conditions are not fulfilled, the indulgence will be partial only.

27. The three conditions may be fulfilled several days before or after the performance of the prescribed work; it is, however, fitting that Communion be received and the prayer for the intention of the Sovereign Pontiff be said on the same day the work is performed.

28. A single sacramental confession suffices for gaining several plenary indulgences; but Communion must be received

---

[47] Taken from *Enchiridion of Indulgences: Norms and Grants*. Catholic Book Publishing. New York. 1969.

and prayer for the intention of the Sovereign Pontiff must be recited for the gaining of each plenary indulgence.

29. The condition of praying for the intention of the Sovereign Pontiff is fully satisfied by reciting one *Our Father* and one *Hail Mary*; nevertheless, each one is free to recite any other prayer according to his piety and devotion.

Made in United States
Orlando, FL
06 November 2025